A Journey in Love

Alissa Barragan-Lancaster

BookLeaf Publishing

India | USA | UK

A Journey in Love © 2024 Alissa Barragan-Lancaster

All rights reserved.

No part of this publication may be reproduced, stored in a retrieval system, or transmitted, in any form or by any means, electronic, mechanical, photocopying, recording or otherwise, without the prior written permission of the presenters.

Alissa Barragan-Lancaster asserts the moral right to be identified as author of this work.

Presentation by *BookLeaf Publishing*

Web: www.bookleafpub.com

E-mail: info@bookleafpub.com

ISBN: 9789360946210

First edition 2024

*To the happy, the hopeful, the heartbroken,
and the healing.*

Contained

I
Hold
Back
So
Much.

Don't we all?

Forgotten

It was hours ago, I walked into the garage and
closed the door behind.
I can't recall what I was looking for when I got
trapped inside.
I banged and screamed and pulled that door, and
the whole time I cried.
I don't know why it wouldn't open, but I tried
and tried and tried.

Was it my heart or was it my mind that broke
first when you weren't there?
Why had you not found me yet and did you even
care?
When it got dark, why weren't you worried that
I had not come home?
Can you imagine how it felt to be stuck in there
alone?

Every night, you went outside to put the dog
away.
That's when you found me, in the garage, where
I had been all day.
"How didn't you know that I was missing?" I
asked leaving my tomb.
"I'm sorry" was all that you could say. "I
thought you were in your room."

Unspoken Words

I have these unspoken words
Like a blister in my mouth.
Acknowledgement is to suffer the ache.
To think is to doubt.
How long has this been here?
And, will this sensation pass?
If I push, poke and prod
Will these words amass?
Will they be known to only me,
Felt only by my tongue?
Or will they be cheered and celebrated,
Like a war finally won?
I guess I'll have to accept the sting
Of these words that won't come out.
For they plague my mind incessantly
And to think is to doubt.

Drunkin' Love- Part 1

Arms wrapped around your waist
Your little stumbles, filled with grace
A playful smile on your face
Baby, I just want a taste

Lips pressed against your shoulder
Your body's warm, the world's colder
You love how I'm getting bolder
Here, for you, my heart will smolder

Make our way up winding stairs
Heart skipping beats, but I'm not scared
I want you naked, your chest bared
We'll do things you never dared

True Love's Table

5

Dinner is served, our eyes alight,
As we smile across the table.
Listening to music, sharing this time,
Has become an honored staple.

We eat, we joke, we sing along
Until our dinner's done.
Then we sit alone, playing cards,
As night forces out the sun.

You never played cards when you were young;
So, for me, it was a treat.
Watching you learn and improve and win
Became a nightly feat.

Our friendship grew around that table
And from that time I knew;
My love for you is never-ending.
My love for you is true.

Daniella

Your beautiful brown eyes peer through my
glass. My heart is clear to see.
Its rhythm in sync with the sound of Alanis, that
comes from the TV.
You know it well, that brilliant pink form that
beats here in my chest.
You watch it like a hawk in flight, never in need
of rest.
The lightest change in color or tempo alarms
your anxious nature.
Is there something I'm not saying? Is my heart a
traitor?
Trust me dear, it's only you who sees the glass
and can peer through.
The others don't matter. They cannot see. My
heart's for only you, Darling.

Drunkin' Love- Part 2

Throw you down on a soft white sheet
Removing shoes from tired feet
You pull me up, as our lips meet
Your kiss like candy, sticky sweet

Kissing you, I can hardly breathe
Teeth that bite and tongues that tease
After pulling down your jeans
I'm begging to go to my knees

Your body calls me, like a song
Your curves a tune, I sing along
The things you say, your message strong
Your thighs are shaking and mind is gone

I lie here waiting, let you recover
I'm a kind and gracious lover
I still feel your body shudder
Come on baby, I want another

Love Lies Below

Quick to leap, slow to fall
I race towards the expanse.
"What an exciting time!" I think
As I bound towards our chance.
When I first saw you, I never thought
I'd find what we have now.
I'd be surprised to hear
that you even noticed me around.
But something told me, "Get to know her."
She's more than she seems.
I can't quite say yet who you are.
I hardly know your dreams.
For the first me ever, here I float
over this chasm called love.
But I'm not scared to glide awhile;
for now, that is enough.
I've learned much more than many have
about love and loss and grief.
And though I can see love below,
I can't see underneath.
Will I let myself settle, slowly down,
into this canyon so near?
No, I think I'll have to wait
and see if you appear.

Betrayed

She's been through it all, another, after
another, after another broken heart.
But you see her now, this independent
Queen, an exemplary work of art.
And you wish you hadn't been the one
to start this lttle trend,
of tearing her down and smashing her
dreams, as she's betrayed again.
Now, she's tired of the calls, the texts,
the "Where do we go from here?"
She wants to scream out "Go to Hell!"
as she holds back a tear.
You can't have now, this perfect life,
you didn't want back then.
You should have loved her when you had her,
because now you're just a friend.

The Walk

If you think this was a happy walk, it wasn't.
It was a walk of sadness. A walk of loneliness.
A walk of emptiness. There was a
need for space. Space from all things.
Space from sound and space from quiet.
Space from love and space from indifference.
Space from awareness and
space from the unacknowledged.

This was a walk meant to heal, but it didn't.
This walk hurt. This walk ripped at
bandages that were already peeling away.
This walk created animosity where there
once was unbridled love. This walk brought
questions
in a basket that should have been full of roses.

The Overthinker

Words have always meant a lot
I have an eager ear
Caged alone as only thought
Their meaning seems unclear

So, I speak the words I can't keep inside
Or else they'll go amiss
They fill my mind up through the night
And rob my dreams of bliss

Tell me your thoughts and share your feelings
I long to understand
Are your heart and head both reeling
Trying to make amends?

As I seek your presence and voice
Fear grips my weary soul
For what you say, and what I hear
Are out of my control

My eager ears betray me
As they turn your words to pain
And disappointment overwhelms
As it fills my aching brain

If Things Never Changed

If things never changed
I could keep you forever.
We'd be just like this
Nothing worse, nothing better.

When you'd look in my eyes
You would still see me here.
You'd miss all the emptiness
I feel drawing near.

I'd play my part
Writing words on this page.
We'd never get sick
And we'd never age.

We'd live in our worlds
Both together, but alone.
Our little talks would start
As soon as I got home.

Together in the world
But I'd feel estranged.
That's how it'd be
If things never changed.

It's Too Late

You've had all this time
        to show me
               what's important
                       to you.

And now that
        I'm gone,
               you've decided
                       it's me.

Just Tell Me

I'm sorry, but I'm confused.
How is this affecting you?

I've got friends in higher places;
Beautiful, bright smiles and warm embraces.
But it's your approval my heart chases.
My mind's shifting like the moon through
phases.

You're not asking how I feel.
Without you, can my heart heal?
I'm asking, was the friendship real?
Your walls arose, as hard as steel.

Get a Therapist

You said that you'd be here for me,
but it did not take long
for me to look around and see
that, clearly, you were gone.

You said you cared for both of us,
but then you turned your back.
As a friend, you had my trust,
now my heart is out of whack.

You said that we need me alone
to decide just what we want.
Now I'm stuck here, in my own mind,
wondering if this was all a front.

You said, "A therapist would help"
Just the second time we talked.
I took it as "Go fuck yourself"
and that was when you walked.

I've begged for you to come around
and start acting like my friend.
I tell myself to let you go,
and then I beg again.

All These Questions

How do I tell you what I need? Can't you see it
in my eyes?
If I laid my heart before you, would you be
surprised?
Does my tone of voice confuse you? Am I too
stern? Am I too quiet?
Are you looking at me now and thinking "Yeah,
she's alright?"
Does being too close to me feel like a chore?
Will you think I'm too greedy if I'm asking for
more?
Is there time in your schedule? Are you too busy
to care?
Do you think it'd be easier if I wasn't there?
Were we ever really close? Was I desperate to
see,
only the parts of you that looked just like me?
How do I not feel disappointed? Should I not be
let down?
Would it even matter if I wasn't around?
If you chose sides, would you tell me? Would
you leave me here guessing?
Will you send me away, on my own, with a
blessing?
Is it possible to stay here in this house divided?

Have minds been made up? Have you already
decided?
What if I don't want to lose you? What if this
isn't fair?
Is it easier to leave when you see my blank
stare?
Does this whole thing confuse you? Is it hard to
believe
that the hardest thing for me is to say what I
need?

Beginnings Come From Ends

After weeks of worrying, I realized,
It wasn't me who hurt you.
It was her, that blonde-haired girl,
Who stole your trust and desire to

To be loved and cherished by another,
Is not a welcome thought.
You fear that you might find another
Who won't value what you

You brought to the table
A soul so strong, you were shocked to see it
bend.
But, I'm here to remind you
That beginnings come from ends.

Loneliness Will Not Last

All I can say is
Loneliness will not last.
In this life,
Some will lecture,
Stating life's purpose is to find
Another person, a soulmate,
Bound to be joined through life and beyond.
And you will listen, and you will look;
Rummaging through bins. Frantically searching
for The
Right One. The one who will overtake your
mind.
And those who seek shall find.
Given time, love will come to
All. And with love comes loss and learning.
Never has a soul felt the fiery brilliance of
Love without
Adventuring through the excruciating pain of
heartache.
Now hearts and minds, at times, do
Clash. Why so much pain when I want them so
bad?
Alone, unpaired, how does one
Survive?
Time is our friend, teacher, healer.
Endless opportunities await.
Remember, loneliness will not last.

Unrequited

I refuse to fall alone.
I've been there too many times.
I see the patterns. I know the words.
I've memorized the signs.

I'm tougher than I used to be.
I'd accept the little I got.
I'd wait for you to catch the feelings
I'd already caught.

So, I'm not going to stand here, idle;
you reaping the benefits of my love.
I'm heading to go find myself,
And I'm hoping that's enough.

Help

I've
Become
Buried

So deeply

Beneath the words in my head

That I don't know

If I'll ever escape.

What I Wish I Knew

My mom never warned me that I would get hurt.
My lessons were learned when my face marred
with dirt.
I raced down our hill with my hands in the air,
Peddling faster than most kids would dare.
A few trips down that hill ended in pain.
Despite the blood and bruises, I'd hop on again.

My mom never taught me when enough is
enough.
She handled my dad, although the marriage was
rough.
I saw what she had, and I thought "Me... marry?
Never!"
I'd escape heartache, and my life could be better.

My mom never showed me how to repair what is
damaged.
I didn't learn how my emotions were managed.
There were very few arguments that I ever
heard.
But my dad could destroy us with barely a word.

I had to teach myself; dirty, heartbroken, and
destroyed,
That pain, heartache, and damage weren't things
I could avoid.
My experience and strength have grown
throughout time.
I see now that my happiness is not a crime.

So, I want to teach others how I learned to live,
laugh, and love.
I'll help them to grow and to rise above.
Because life's really hard when you grow up
without guidance.
I want our lives to be plentiful. I don't just want
to survive this.

www.ingramcontent.com/pod-product-compliance
Lightning Source LLC
LaVergne TN
LVHW050257200726

843509LV00015B/3065